E8

Barbaresi & Round
Emily Cole
Tom Hunter
Hilary Jack
Gary O'Connor
Laura Oldfield Ford
Matthew Stock
walkwalkwalk

E8: The Heart of Hackney
16 June – 15 July 2007 Transition Gallery London

Published in 2007 by Transition Editions
Unit 25a Regent Studios, 8 Andrews Road, London E8 4QN

Transition Editions is the publishing wing of Transition Gallery
E8 The Heart of Hackney is Edition 005

ISBN 0-9548954-4-4

Edited by Cathy Lomax
Designed by Yolanda Zappaterra
Printed by Aldgate Press

Cover Image: Tom Hunter: 'London Fields' from the 'Swansongs' series

With thanks to Ian Graham. This publication has been made possible with the support of Arts Council England, Awards For All, London Metropolitan University, Norwich School of Art & Design and Thames Valley University

CONTENTS

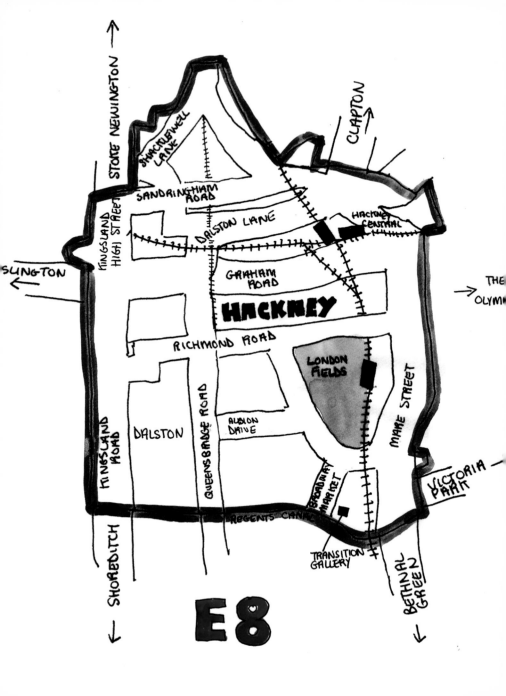

Drifting and Shifting

The Royal Mail started assigning postcodes in the UK in 1959; they were convenient ways of sorting the mail into geographical areas and had little significance beyond this. East London postcodes start with an E and E8 is the code that Transition Gallery just happens to be in. Since this low-key introduction, postcodes have become much more than arbitrary mail districts and have taken on the significant task of defining local identities. In London a code will immediately position you on the social ladder, something that has taken on a sinister twist in East London where postcode gangs defend their territories. Step over the invisible line between E5 and E9 and 'bang bang' as the graffiti goes, may just become a reality.

In 2004 Transition Gallery was located in Lauriston Road, E9. Keen to show our commitment to the area I curated a show called E9: An Anatomy of an Area, which featured work by Clive Brandon, Tania McCormack, Gary O'Connor and Mike Perry. When we relocated to Regent Studios, E8 in 2006 I decided to apply this same concept to our new location and thus E8: The Heart of Hackney was born.

The eight artists involved in E8 have all approached the area in different ways, from a micro concentration on the building the gallery occupies to broader views that sweep through E8 and drift into Victoria Park and Hackney Wick. This publication adds an extra dimension to the exhibition with texts on the artists and the area by Juliette Adair, I. Dunnop, Ruth Jarvis, Charlie Porter, Angela Ravetz and Iain Sinclair.

Celebrating the local is something that seems increasingly important in the fast-changing landscape of East London where the Olympics and gentrification are destroying everything in their path leaving small isolated pockets of poverty behind as the masses are pushed out to the near suburbs. I hope that the E8 project will add to your understanding and enjoyment of this rapidly changing area of London.

Cathy Lomax, Director of Transition Gallery

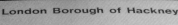

London Borough of Hackney

Mare Street E8

E8: A Modern Mess
By Charlie Porter. Photos by Mike Talbot

E8, that bastardised postcode. But bastardised from what? E8 was cut a bum deal when the London boundaries were drawn. It is defined by the traffic arteries of the Kingsland Road, Queensbridge Road, Mare Street and those thin failures of roads through Dalston that prevent the area from ever feeling purposeful. The postcode's focus is the administrative heart of Hackney Council, a lingering national joke. One border north, Stoke Newington gives N16 an air of bumbling, satisfied cosiness. East, previous Transition fodder E9 has more sense of tradition. But E8 doesn't even know what it was before it became the modern mess that it is now.

E8's saving fallback is London Fields. 'It is not a park, but common land,' says Tom Hunter, who is showing at E8 an image of the Fields at night, 'a stop-off for flocks of sheep being herded to London markets, so it never closes.' Fitting that the postcode's main space should feel lawless. Indeed, the shape of the borough mimics the outline of the Fields itself, as if the borough is an extension of its prized, rudderless asset. 'For over 20 years I've lived within 100 yards of the Fields, in eight different flats or houses,' says Hunter. 'It's where I have always gone to meet up with my friends on a summer evening. Somewhere to play football, frisbee, baseball and even volleyball for a few summers. It has also acted as a venue, where you can take your own drinks and sit out underneath a nuclear pink and red light-polluted sky.'

Hunter's image taps the fear that still seeps the Fields, even though its south edge leads to Broadway Market, E8's area of sudden, sharp gentrification. 'Walking across the park's open spaces after dark becomes a gamble with life itself,' he says. 'This violence is all but forgotten now on a sunny Saturday afternoon on Broadway Market, where the boarded up and derelict buildings have been transformed into havens for latte-swilling mums and their 4x4 buggies, with talk of dole queues and violence drowned out by tales of huge property deals and profits.' Which gets to the crux of this uneasy social shift: sneering is easy at life-by-Farmers-Market, but who has fondness for the social malaise it now overrides?

Emily Cole has an outsider view of E8, a visitor to the area from Norwich. 'My excursions to E8 involved me feeling like a tourist trying to find her way around a foreign place, map in hand,' says Cole. 'In fact, thinking about all this makes me wonder whether my impressions of E8 are dominated by trying to negotiate my way round the area by bus or on foot, usually getting a bit lost and self-conscious staring into my A-Z, which unfortunately has no map that indicates where E8 starts and ends. I was forever looking at street signs to figure out whether I was in E8, E9 or E2.' It's these walks that led to the paintings she is showing at E8, which pay particular attention to leisure in the area, recently re-energised by the re-opening of the London Fields Lido. 'Last November I persuaded my brother to go for a swim there on a Sunday morning,' she says. 'It was bright and sunny and there were autumn leaves floating around in the water which was not too cold considering it was November. And as we left after our swim there was a huge queue of people waiting to get into the pool which got me thinking how this oasis of fresh air and water is really used by a lot of people in the neighbourhood - in fact, they probably need three or four lidos, not just one.'

Cole's overriding impression of E8 is that of a knot. 'I can't really compare E8 to Norwich as it is so different,' she says. 'E8 seems more tangled up, I see it as having dilapidated warehouses with dodgy looking side streets, and falling down houses near to new build flats, probably for people

London Borough of Hackney

Graham Road E8

working in the city – and then round the corner from all this there might be
a sedate Victorian square like the one on Albion Drive complete with water
fountain, even though it's not working.'

This knot is something that the walkwalkwalk collective gleefully exploit.
Clare Qualmann, Serena Korda and Gail Burton have mapped a path between
the chip shops of E8, making seemingly meaningless tracks across the district
that actually reveal tales of flux and hardship, social change and personal
history. Walkwalkwalk have spoken with the establishments, leaving their
chip forks at each for walkers to collect. During the process, they have been
told many realities of what is presumed to be an English institution – that
tradition rarely exists in aspic. If it does, like at F Cooke's Pie and Mash shop
on Broadway Market, it sits at stark odds with what is happening all around.

What is it of E8 that is being left high and dry by the drive to
gentrification? Barbaresi & Round have been interviewing the senior
residents of the borough to provide some sort of context, creating work at
Transition that runs alongside the oral histories collected by the artists.
'There is a sense from the interviews that pre-war and during the war there
was a settled community,' says Susanna Round, who partners with Rachel
Barbaresi. 'Although after the war there were major changes in the area due
to slum clearance and building projects to tackle the housing crisis, it seems

London Borough of Hackney

Malpas Road E8

that it was the movement of people, and the consequential 'break-up of the community' that made the biggest impact on E8.'

Hilary Jack is also engaged in the idea of memory, although her dint is towards the pointlessness of artefact. 'I think I am short-circuiting the end, the death of these objects,' she says. For her work, Jack finds then repairs items, before returning them to their original location. Often these repairs are beneficial, but for E8 she is being purposefully ineffectual: a tennis racquet found in Hackney is re-strung like macramé, a football repatched using leather cuts from a workshop in Regents Studio. 'My personal investment in these objects is huge, as I often go to great lengths to get the objects repaired, learning a new skill or paying someone else to help me in the task,' she says. Her interventions look at the naïve hope for the micro to affect the macro. 'It is a futile act as it is so minimal and ineffectual in the grand scheme of things,' she says, 'as are our own efforts as a community when considering how huge the problem of our waste management is and how multi-national companies and governments worldwide can be found flouting environmental efforts.'

Others have fierce opinions about the district. In her writings for fanzine Savage Messiah, Laura Oldfield Ford mixes cultural theory with a political outlook, counteracted with her own dreamy drawings. Meanwhile

Matthew Stock has set up surveillance cameras around Regent Studio to beam images of the block into Transition Gallery. 'Over the past decade we have been led to believe that our cities are in a constant state of war,' he says. 'We as citizens have been told to always be aware of the threat. We need to protect ourselves. I for one wonder, why?'

Stock is interested in the link between surveillance cameras and location. 'Take the concourse level at Tottenham Court Road station,' he says. 'There are surveillance systems in place that will track your movements through, within and around the concourse. If your movements do not follow a pre-determined norm a signal is sent to the Underground police and they are dispatched to investigate. Yet surveillance can only detect the location that you inhabit at the present time. It cannot know your intended location in the future or indeed in the past.'

By making his location Regent Studios itself, Stock is documenting a particular extremity of E8. Transition Gallery not only sits on the border of the postcode's boundary, it also sits on the edge of Hackney itself. Regent Studios is a brutal building that looms over the Regent Canal – a modern day fortress with its dirty watered moat. 'It is as if the canal is protecting E8,' says Stock. 'It would have once been the trade route for business and communication, but it would also have defined a way of life and a

community. Now it sits in its twilight years kind of disregarded, almost lonely, maybe thinking back to its heyday. It does of course have a role within today's modern age and it is about protecting but also about defining.'

Stock is not the only E8 contributor to use Regent Studios as its source material. Gary O'Connor uses his experience of once getting trapped in the Regent Studios lift as the starting place for his purposefully twisted work. 'As an artist and a writer, the aspect of location plays an important role in my work,' says O'Connor. 'A sense of place, its history and the people who live and work there become subjects of inquiry. In terms of structure; I try not to constrict myself: pushing the envelope and breaking convention is at the heart of what I do, although this may not always be apparent at first glance. Sometimes this means pulling the carpet out from under my own feet: facts become blurred, exaggerated, and riddled with contradiction.'

Just like E8 itself. Indeed Regent Studio is full of the bustle and hum that shows the district at its best, as it ought to be. 'Regent Studios is an environment that is changing,' says Matthew Stock. 'More artists and galleries are moving in, taking advantage of the space and its close proximity to the Vyner Street gang. There is a creative shift, and I often wonder at any one time how much creativity is taking place in that building.' Or, indeed, postcode.

EMILY COLE

Making Pretty: Emily Cole as urban tourist. By Iain Sinclair

Previous page: Emily Cole, 'Local Mutt Study' 2007, sump oil on paper. Opposite: Emily Cole, 'Parking' 2007, oil, acrylic and sump oil on board.

On the grey stone slabs of Warneford Street, an interestingly unresolved tributary of King Edwards Road in Hackney, someone has chalked a grid of hopscotch figures: all of them E9. Thereby making a chessboard of the narrow pavement - and, by extension, of the city. Dangerous additives. On other sites this assertion of identity, the branding war between E9 and E8, would be a tribal challenge akin to slinging a pair of trainers over sagging telephone lines. The precise definition of territorial boundaries can become a matter of life and death.

Chalk is mortal, it crumbles in the mouth. Cemeteries of ancient marine life become the quarries of southern England, sculpted into retail parks, off-highway Bluewater shopping oases. The enamel-stripping shriek of chalk on blackboard. Heritage schoolrooms where we learnt by rote, by copying meaningless formulae. It invokes that rubbed out Willem de Kooning drawing: there and not there, always there. A smeary action-gesture of strategic removal. Chalk symbols and faked York-stone pavings, coming together in Warneford Street, demonstrate a potent urban myth. The temporary-permanent intervention of an anonymous artist and the permanent-temporary nature of civic improvement (slabs breaking up before they are laid in place).

Without this random equation how would a stranger locate herself in a constantly shifting East London geography? Old-time tramps and vagrants chalked symbols on pavings and doors, their private code: generous, mean or dog-threatening households. Now unsponsored artists sign the city. Their practice is about recognition rather than aesthetic colonialisation. You like it, you sign it. There is no requirement to bring anything home. No collaboration with the commissioning process (which has become the principal art form of the Blair era). No armature of curatorship, grant application, ludicrous explanations of future events (that will never come into being). No tyranny of political correctness. No value. Until, of course, in zones hysterical with self-consciousness, guerrilla art is puffed into cash art. Trashed buildings and disregarded walls are prepared for property speculation by the imprimatur of a Banksy stencil. And then you have the ironic spectacle of cleansing operations (compulsory in over-budgeted, upwardly mobile development areas) being taken to task for the vandalism of painting over earlier vandalism – which itself covered up some faded Edwardian trade sign for violin repairs, barbering or the cure of love's wounds. The age of the scavenger is over and rubbish is just rubbish: unless you can

persuade a gallery to give it floorspace.

Emily Cole is a product of East Anglia; born in Ipswich, educated in Cambridge, living and working in Norwich. Her car has a hook on the back to drag a trailer with a canoe on board. You see at once, by the way she navigates the discriminations of Hackney, that she is happiest with water, with parks (those 'green lungs' bestowed on the urban poor). Emily's London A-Z has no truck with cultural contour lines. The speed and fret of the city disorientates her. She's willing to make a painterly grid of E8 – if she can find it. Her awkwardness with mapping is justified, original settlements grew up around natural features such as the vanished (suppressed) Hackney Brook; E-numbers are arbitrary inventions of bureaucrats and politicians carving up territory.

She suffers. On Brick Lane, a mild ruck develops between some young Asians peddling mobile phones and a man with a camera. You have to learn, very quickly, about the paranoia of image making. Cameras are more threatening than guns (which are now accessories). When Emily, struggling to get a fix on this E8 thing, this shapeless wilderness, used an old prose journey of mine as a guide, she got as far as Dalston Junction before the presence of her digital camera provoked a direct confrontation. As the whole borough has become a CCTV movie, logged on monitor screens in a former library, so the citizens – in revenge – have turned on humble analogue technology, the flash of the amateur topographer. A woman taking a photograph of a car shunt on Kingsland Road was punched in the mouth and told by the police that it was

her own fault. Image making, it appears, is a more serious form of assault than some good old-fashioned GBH. Images are also property. And property, in E8, is the ultimate value. If you have it, you can't afford it. If you don't have it, you never will. You don't belong and it's time you moved out. To Dagenham, Grays or Hackney-on-Sea (aka Hastings).

The initial research undertaken by Emily Cole is in some ways the most intriguing part of her project. She wandered the streets, accosting strangers at bus stops, on benches beside the canal, and inscribed her notes on the large-format digital portraits. She did not paint from the motif or make instant sketches. She carried her photographs back to the safety and calm of her Norwich studio. The human figures – a junk dealer

with a fondness for music hall, a celebrity mum with a son marooned on Love Island – vanish. They don't make it into the final E8 grid. They are effectively banished like the lowlife that once animated Jock McFadyen's paintings of Limehouse Cut and Bethnal Green. Personality is subsumed into place. With some relief, Emily decides to structure her work around sites the E8 denizens drift towards as a retreat from pressure, from dirt and noise. She stakes out Victoria Park, that fabulous narrative, a blot of lush greenery ceded by Hackney to Tower Hamlets. An act of pure folly forced on a hapless and indigent council. Like the giving up, by the French, of Alsace-Lorraine.

Those research tools, the digital photos and cyberspace retrievals of a virtual Hackney, are bigger than Emily Cole's postcard-like blocks of paintings. She works in units of six: reminding me of the paving stones of Warneford Street, as if they had errupted into ecstatic colour. A 'zingy' acrylic base with overpainting in oil. The scheme built around lively pinks and greens. Cole's pink is like Caladryl lotion splashed on sunburnt grass and post-nuclear brick. She decided to manoeuvre around the fixed geometry of monuments, celebrating their obscurity, the fact that they were now memorials to a loss of memory, amnesiac stalagmites. Worthy causes, forgotten battles, suspended charities: all gone, time-absolved, erased like chalk inscriptions on wet pavements.

The texture of Cole's paint is anti-chalk, it's strident, eye-gouging. She sets herself to redeem blight, to 'make pretty'. The brick plinth on which Victoria Park's damaged guardians, the 'Dogs of Alcibiades', sit, doesn't appeal to her – so she fleshes it into a liquid, cocktail pink. The demonic addition, 666, gifted by some juvenile occultist, has been cartooned in Loony Toon colour. The park's lakeside café is squished into an ice-cream cone yurt, its concrete surround rendered as a cadmium-flush beach. One of the stone igloos, removed from old London Bridge, is revamped into an arbour with a young lady perched on the bench (which the artist has tactfully restored). Here is an improved city, an arcadia wrestled from gritty particulars. An old, arthritic borough ready to be face-painted in provincial gloss. E8, in the hands of Emily Cole, is a suburb of itself. 'Where are the green places?' she asks me. 'Where are the statues?' The surreal Pearly Kings and Queens. The black marble tributes to

murdered policemen. The horse troughs full of Coke cans and ring pulls.

Checking out the Alcibiades legend, the Norwich artist discovers some business about docking the dog's tail – so she runs this conceit through to a local mutt, presented on the canal bank, beside the boho owner's narrowboat. Cole's E8 is 'rescued', returned to its bucolic origin of market gardens and grand houses with estates running down to the lost Hackney Brook. When these brightly painted panels move beyond the recording of specifics into free-flowing abstraction, they echo Ivon Hitchens. They become ambiguous, otherworldly, tunnels of wild light. Thrusting stone memorials are hermaphroditic upthrusts with mammary decoration. Fountains are dry. Nature is de-natured. The most reflective of the drawings, pitched towards sepia, like friable photographs found in a street market, are made with sump oil; a lovely marriage of grunge and water-light. Impressionist subject matter revisited in a machine age.

Alcibiades the Athenian, whose dogs have been vandalised in Victoria Park, faces smashed, overpainted with the devil's number, was himself accused of mutilating statues. Androcles fabricated evidence against him when all the heads of Hermes within the city, perched on their plinths, were damaged overnight. The Eleusinian Mysteries had been profaned. Alcibiades, before standing trial, sailed away on a military expedition. He was a convinced advocate of an aggressive foreign policy. Statues topple, regimes change: the need remains for somebody to paint the postcards that send back hot news from the ravished city.

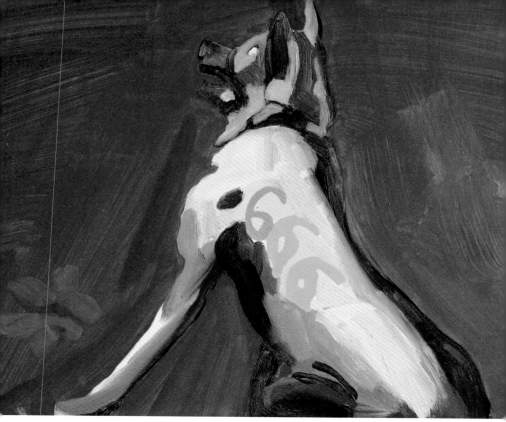

Previous spread: Emily Cole, 'Canalside' 2007, oil
and acrylic on board (left); Emily Cole, 'Waterway'
2007, oil, acryic and sump oil on board. Above: Emily
Cole, 'Dog of Alcibiades (Occult)', oil and acrylic on
board. All paintings 16.5cm x 21.5cm.

LAURA OLDFIELD FORD

"The universal and ineluctable consequence of this crusade to secure the city is the destruction of accessible public space. The contemporary opprobrium attached to the term 'street person' is itself a harrowing index of the devaluation of public spaces. To reduce contact with untouchables, urban redevelopment has converted once vital pedestrian streets into traffic sewers and transformed public parks into temporary receptacles for the homeless and wretched. The American city, as many critics have recognised, is being systematically turned inside out- or rather outside in. The valorized spaces of the new megastructures and supermalls are concentrated in the centre, street frontage is denuded, public activity is sorted into strictly functional compartments, and circulation is internalized in corridors under the gaze of private police."

Mike Davis City of Quartz

The Dalston masterplan, pore over glossily photoshopped projections of retail park and new town square, a panoptican monad ,consumer avatars operating ghoulishly under the supervision of a giant plastic Ronald and a hundred hidden cameras. Who runs this future zone, whose rules are we expected to live by? Behind the mocking Gacey grin of every Ronald there's a hundred sneering marines patrolling US gulags around the world. The burger stink that clogs the street becomes a signifier of decay. A banal Americanisation sweeps the planet. Public space is rapaciously eroded , shut in and privately 'managed'. Group 4 armies enforce laws banning loitering, photography, smoking and drinking in the name of anti social behaviour or prevention of terror. Sensory filtering and environmental manipulation ensures the outside world is a dim memory, successfully erased, aren't we lucky to be here now?

We exist in a perpetual state of emergency, immured in a
that can never end.

TODAY'S GATED COMMUNITIES, TOMORROWS GULAGS!!!!!!!!!!!!

Small acts of everyday sabotage, a jamming of codes, the scrambling and subverting of space, spanners thrown into the works, this is the way we hit back at this magic lantern show of grotesqueries.

Drifting through Dalston is to traverse a network of holdi
patterns, a city in stasis, it is a series of film still
waiting rooms, a life behind it and another yet to come.
the fabric of the architecture I uncover traces a
palimpsests, the poly-temporality of the city. As I lay my pa
flat against the wall I buffer multiple traces of pa
workings and reworkings, the polychromatic riot of London
histories travel in shimmering, tangled lines.

WANKERS.
Boring middle class wankers!!!!!!! stop moving into Hackney
and demanding restrictions on boozing antics, ultra violence
or any other street activity that makes it a good place to
live. Move back to Surrey or whatever miserable home counties
enclave you come from!! We are bored of your naked self
interest!! You push house prices up, moan about proles and
contribute FUCK ALL!!!!!!!!!!!!

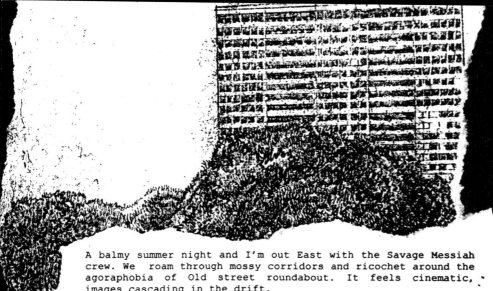

A balmy summer night and I'm out East with the Savage Messiah crew. We roam through mossy corridors and ricochet around the agoraphobia of Old street roundabout. It feels cinematic, images cascading in the drift.

You remember that afternoon in the foundry? Warm rain, schizoid weather, everyone locked in for the afternoon. And we were in that corner, faces magenta in the neon. It was Bank holiday, no one giving a fuck about anything but getting wrecked, one of those mad afternoon sessions where everyone's running round the boozer like it's their own private party, threshold between thinking and acting dissolving in the mayhem.

On the pints, looking hectically better with each one, some kid playing Cabaret Voltaire records, scratchy and distorted, boot sale treasure, voices resurrected from an attic burial. Rain eases off, soft vapour rises from the streets, a battered transit, 2000 DS graffitied on the side ,skids off the roundabout and onto the pavement in front of the pub. A crew of anarcho deviants bundle out the back. Straight over to the decks, post punk kid thrown back into the crowd as they commandeer with an unholy clash of Flux of Pink Indians and demented clown tech. Our neon corner is colonised by the crew, who have the military fatigues and shaven heads of Spiral Tribe. This lot are hardcore. You know any of them?

Where you lot from?
Hackney Wick.

Some of the streets down there right, they aint even on the map, they aint even got names, all them little streets running through the estates, terra incognita. Pallet citadels, avenues of portakabins, transient architecture emerging, unfolding and wrapping up again, no one even knows it's there, and that's how we like it.

We're all pretty off it now, and one of these lads has just passed round a bottle of mushroom tea so you know , you can imagine, we're totally wrecked, pissing ourselves over fuck all. Someone kisses me, beat up skinhead, face a lattice work of scars, nice one, no one gives a fuck.

Crew in fine form now, bawling shouting kind of pissed up, everyone's on side and we got the whole boozer, all we need now to round things off is a mass brawl. I lead the mob onwards in search of cheap thrills and ultra violence.

DEVELOPERS!!HACKNEYCOUNCIL!!YUPPIES!HANDS OFF OUR ESTATES!!!!
FUCK OFF TO THE THAMES GATEWAY!!!!!!!!!

HILARY JACK
The In-betweeness of Things
By Amanda Ravetz

A pair of leather shoes on a bus stop bench, a torn football by a bin, a wooden tennis racquet propped against the wall. Hilary Jack's matter-of-fact images evoke the journeys objects take towards obsolescence, suggesting an easy-come, easy-go attitude to mass-produced goods. And yet a melancholy hangs over these discarded bits of lives, evocative of human loss and of how the shedding of things leaves us strangely diminished. Once they are broken, we can no longer take them for granted; they disturb and unsettle us.

Jack not only photographs discarded and lost objects, she brings them back from the brink. The leather shoes have been repaired, polished and embossed with golden words. The football re-stitched and inflated. The racquet has been made fit for a new purpose, migrating from the street to the gallery.

At a time when local authorities in the UK are making the recycling of household waste compulsory, this work has a particular resonance. Local government websites explain the (complicated) arrangements residents must follow in sorting their waste into colour-coded boxes. They list the collection times, the types of vehicle and equipment that will remove the bottles, plastic and tins. Turning attention to more idiosyncratic items, Jack's work also references the excesses of an economy based on built-in-obsolescence. And yet the very bathos of her gestures provokes the thought that recycling itself may be a futile action in the face of so much consumption and waste.

Indeed it is through the possibility of failure—the futility of the repairs carried out, the possibility that the replaced objects will not survive—that Jack's work lodges its appeal. There is no guarantee that the things that have been cleaned or repaired and returned to the places where they were found will re-enter the social worlds they left. And so, cut adrift from their pasts,

Hilary Jack 'Make do and Mend' 2006: Top to bottom, left to right: Found shoes; Cleaning the shoes; Restored and gilded left shoe; Replaced found shoes

their futures uncertain, their very in-betweeness invites curiosity about their trajectories—and about other inanimate things.

Running through avant-garde theory is a strong belief in the purposelessness of art. The power of the aesthetic encounter lies in its freedom from instrumentality, evoking in turn a future free of human self-interest. By taking the everyday into the social world of art, the relationships surrounding objects are gently re-aligned, their purposes changed.

Jack's work causes utilitarian items to reveal a side of themselves beyond their practical usefulness, their original journeys, or the contexts of their use and abuse. The emblems of sociality that Jack adds in the forms of inscriptions, the other subtle interventions she makes, draw these ordinary objects into another aesthetic domain, and in so doing, insert a tiny pause between purpose and purposelessness.

When the door-closer 'goes on strike', says anthropologist Bruno Latour, we momentarily acknowledge its agency in our world. We speak bitter words when things let us down, investing the things around us with expectations, memory, frustration, hope. Objects are not human, but they are part of our social world.

At the heart of Hilary Jack's work is a commitment to 'the social life of things'. Her gathering and rehabilitation of lost or abandoned objects are less acts of altruism than statements of fact. Holding open the possibility that objects are (non-human) people, treating them as interlocutors, the artist momentarily defies the incommensurability between our world and theirs.

Dr Amanda Ravetz is an AHRC Fellow at MIRIAD, Manchester Metropolitan University where she is currently pursuing research into 'Contemporary Convergence of Aesthetics and Ethnography'.

Maxply

The classic Maxply wooden tennis racket was used by innumerable champions, such as Rod Laver in his 1962 Grand Slam win. Fifty years on the era ended with the 1983 'McEnroe Maxply', the last model to be made. 'Buy one to play with, and one to hang on the wall as a work of art' said the Dunlop advertising slogan.

This abandoned and broken Maxply racket was found leaning casually against a graffitied wall in Hackney; its championship days over as it waited for the street cleaners to arrive and cart it off to landfill.

Rescued from the brink of oblivion by Hilary Jack its fate changed, it was transformed by pins and red thread into an object which mirrors its making and its breaking. Her actions reference the excesses of an economy based on built-in-obsolescence, while the work harks back to bygone days of seventies 'Pin and Thread' craft, of restrung wooden tennis rackets, and of times when our focus was on repair and re-use rather than recycling and waste.

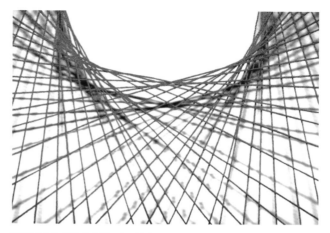

Top: Hilary Jack 'Maxply', 2007, found tennis racket with pins and red thread. Bottom: Hilary Jack 'Maxply' 2007, found tennis racket, Broadway Market Hackney

BARBARESI & ROUND
Homes and Housing

'Hot water, a bathroom, an inside loo, a view over the whole of the city and Victoria Park. We could have a firework display on the Thames, commentary on the radio and we would sit on our balcony with our wine and cheese. It was gorgeous. And in six months it was hell.'

Artists Rachel Barbaresi and Susanna Round are interested in the effects that varying housing stock have on inhabitants - and how they habitate. 'E8 has a unique spectrum of housing, from Georgian townhouse to Victorian terrace to pre-war walk up to post-war tower block to post-welfare state starter home rabbit hutch. We joined a coffee morning at The Building Exploratory in E8 to meet some older residents and talk about some of the dramatic changes in housing over the last 60 years. 'We wanted to know about their memories, opinions, and direct experience of the area.

'Our work uses housing density statistics that have been reconfigured to interpret the use of space in different parts of the postcode. This prompted us to think about the overspill and the move out to respectable suburbs or a new town like Basildon. We have been visiting these places and made some wall drawings using gathered imagery.'

Brenda   I was born on the Kingsmead estate which was built during the war.

Rachel   I wouldn't have thought there was much housing going up during the war.

Susanna   Whereabouts is Kingsmead Estate?

Brenda   Right beside Hackney Marshes. It used to be farmland.

Susanna   So it must be interesting to compare how it was then to how it is now? Do you still live nearby?

Brenda   Not far - I'm now in E8. Well I started in Kingsmead, moved to Morning Lane and then E8. I lived at Kingsmead for thirty odd years and so they're brick built. They're still there whereas some of the new developments that sprung up in the sixties have been demolished but Kingsmead is still standing. 'Walk ups' they used to call them.

Rachel   So they've got the outside walkways?

Bella   They've got balconies. You go up the stairs and then walk along the balconies.

Brenda   The thing about Kingsmead was the size of the rooms. They were good-sized rooms.

Bella   I can remember that people used to be cleaning those stairs.

Above: Barbaresi & Round, Study for 'Basildon', 2007
Below: Brenda and Graham Woods at their home in Mapledene Road, E8

Brenda   You had to.

Bella   You cleaned your windowsills on Friday. You cleaned your doors and your outside loo. And Kingsmead was really in that era wasn't it.

Brenda   Well my mother obviously - cos I was born in '41 - so my mother went into it with my elder brother and elder sister. She died when I was eighteen but I remember her saying that when they moved in as part of the rules you had to take it in turn. So each tenant had to clean down the sixteen stairs to the next landing and you had to keep everything clean.

Rachel   That's amazing. There's really a sense of community in that.

Bella   And then later you found that people didn't want to live in Kingsmead anymore because it wasn't the same. Would you agree?

Brenda   I was a toddler during the war, and everyone was working class and not very well off, but the community pulled together and there wasn't really a lot of crime. We all had our piece of string with the key on it behind the letterbox so when you came home from school you could pull the key out and open the door. It was only as years went by that people changed and people used to shimmy up the drainpipes to get in the back windows, or get in through the front windows because they used to rob

Above: Barbaresi & Round, Study for 'Basildon', 2007
Facing page: Richard and Bella Callaghan, taken at Robin Wood Hill, 1952

	the electric meter or the gas meter. But I got to probably over twenty which would have been about the sixties and then gradually, with the move out of people... Different people came in; whereas we grew up during the war and all the parents... you never knew if you were going to be alive the next day.
Susanna	Do you think that added to the sense of community?
Brenda	I think it did you know. A lot of people had obviously been bombed out and came from dwellings which didn't have an indoor bath or toilet and so it was an improvement for everyone. Gradually I think with the change of people, all different kinds of people, it did become bad.
Rachel	Where were people moving to?
Brenda	Well in those days, people moved out to Chingford and Basildon - new towns - to get out to the country.
Bella	You have to remember, in the days when we had the key on the lock, nobody had anything. You were all the same. And so after the war things changed because there was work, and money started to come in. And people moved out to the new towns that were more affluent.
Susanna	So that makes for greater social divisions.

Bella People had things that could be taken. And then television arrived - well - people could sell that. So people now had possessions that the 'ungodly' as it were, could help themselves to. And that generation found it very difficult to understand why we can't leave our front doors open any more.

Susanna Do you think that happened quite quickly?

Bella I don't know. All the time we lived in the Wick we never had break-ins did we? Until that new development came and then everybody was having them. And even today, we've just had re-development and I've been reminding people, this is when they break in, as they know you've got new things. And they're so clever today that they'll take it this week, and they know next week you're going to get it replaced so they'll come back again.

Rachel And it was people coming from outside the estate?

Bella I don't know that it was, because, you know, you'd got families growing up hadn't you, and their attitudes had changed to the people going before. I can assure you that my daughter is nothing like what we are in the sense that her values are very different.

Rachel So there's no longer that community spirit, and sharing the cleaning of communal areas, and pulling together?

Bella No.

Richard Communities were being broken up because people were being decanted from other parts of town.

Bella GLC brought them in from over the other side of the water - completely different people.

Rachel We've grown up with that. People moving around; our friends going to live in other countries; its assumed that people won't stay in the same place for very long at all. It sounds as though you've lived with the sense that you do stay in the place that you've been brought up. Or perhaps that was just more likely to happen. You were less likely to move around.

Brenda The council or social services started putting in what you would call 'problem families'. Now when you grew up in the war, I had many friends whose fathers had been killed in the war, so they were single parent families as the mums were widowed. Its not a question of single parent families, but problem families were deliberately put in because you had all the people who were living together well and it was working out alright and you put a bad apple in and there's 50 other people, and they're supposed to see how the other people live and become like them. But they just used to make life hell for everyone else.

Bella I totally agree. And it's interesting because we come from completely different parts of Hackney. We lived in the modern tower blocks on the Trowbridge estate in the top floor flat. But we made sure they came down. I went to see them.

Rachel And they've since come down?

Bella Oh I made sure they came down. I went to see them.

Rachel So when you first moved there what were your expectations?

Bella Hot water, a bathroom, an inside loo, a view over the whole of the city and Victoria Park. We could have a firework display on the Thames, commentary on the radio and we would sit on our balcony with our wine and cheese. It was gorgeous. And in six months it was hell. They were prefabs on sticks and they couldn't keep the water out. And when I tell you that one morning we got up because they said it was going to rain and I went into the hall and I screamed "its not raining"... We painted our hall ceiling dark brown, everything else white, because our ceiling, it looked as though there'd been a murder. We had seven bowls collecting oil from the boiler room. You can see why I was incensed enough to talk to my friends and get together...

Susanna When you say 'get together' you mean to get the tower blocks pulled down?

Bella Yes.

Rachel And at what point did you do that? Was it quite soon after they were built?

Bella No, no, no, you tolerate quite a lot don't you. And you don't realize that it's possible to do anything. But then something says 'why don't you'.

Kay When did those blocks come down?

Bella The first one - Northaird block - came down on 3rd November 1985.

Susanna What was the block called that you used to live in?

Bella Deverill Point. But there were seven.

Rachel And they all came down?

Bella Oh yes. Really, a stage in the famous Hamlet cigar advert that came out the day after the demolition. Because it didn't come down. The first one only came down 10 floors.

Susanna Did they do it with dynamite? Down in one?

Bella Yes, and the interesting thing was - no one was hurt - we all stood there crying because it hadn't come down.

Susanna So you were all standing watching the building come down?

Bella Of course.

Richard We were all on the marsh and there were tents with refreshments laid on

	and so on. All of a sudden there was a big bang and dust rolling towards you across the marshes.
Bella	What had happened was, the GLC, we're now Hackney Council because Hackney Council took over in 1982. It was all handed over wasn't it? So we then had to work with the GLC and they had said that they were unsafe. Well of course when it didn't come down they said that one wasn't unsafe. Really they had to come down on social grounds. The anti-social living was incurring big problems.
Rachel	And was it the residents that campaigned for this?
Bella	Yes, it was the residents.
Susanna	Where did you live after that?
Bella	I stayed there didn't I? Because I was so involved in it. You couldn't appear to be running away because they'd say "Oh you're alright now" so you had to stay.
Rachel	So you moved into another building?
Bella	Eventually, in 1985.
Rachel	And you stayed in the same area.
Bella	Oh yes, we wouldn't move out of the area would we Richard?
Richard	I would!
Susanna	So do you feel that it's the structure of the tower block that's the problem, or if a tower block was well maintained and the social elements worked it could be fantastic? You were talking about when you first moved there and you had hot water in your bathroom and how wonderful it was. If things had happened differently could that dream have become a reality?
Bella	I think the different construction might have worked. They were an experimental estate and it depended which way the wind blew whether you would be in trouble today or somebody else. If somebody had, for instance, a leak in the water lets say, now on the 11th floor you'd expect it to affect the 10th, but it might not, it might go down to the 7th. The people on the 7th floor have a leak and that's got to be traced. So they were not a good example of high-rise flats. Once a place had a reputation you couldn't get rid of it. Kingsmead had that problem. But now the Kingsmead residents have taken over as self management and TMC and the money that they've generated with collecting the rents and everything they've put back and in their own way, I'm not sure, but they've made defensible spaces, people have got gardens, and the place is clean again. Because people feel "That's my area". But it takes a long while for that stigma to go.

Susanna	So it's nice to know that things can be turned around.
Brenda	Yes, and that Kingsmead's still standing and the Trowbridge development all had to go.
Bella	But the tenant management - it's the tenants that generated it. Today's residents that have generated it.
Rachel	That's good isn't it. That's very positive.
Bella	You have to remember that when we did this we were young. And to see it happen again is very good.
Brenda	Plus some people have bought the flats under the right to buy so they have more of an interest. I think as well so many people now don't have to pay any rent because obviously they get benefits they're entitled to and its right. But sometimes they've got no feeling in the housing, they don't really care. They don't care if its dirty or whatever. But if you love your home... Because some of the estates, people say "I wouldn't want to live there", but the people that have lived there for a time, they keep their homes nice and look after them, and when you get people saying, "Oh, I wouldn't move in there", you think "but they're not bad people living there". It just gets a reputation. I suppose both Trowbridge wand Kingsmead, they're both on Hackney Marshes, you've got wide spaces, you're not right near built up spaces, it's an ideal situation.

Tex Marsh: one man's E8 story

Susanna: Tex could you tell us about some of your experiences of the area and how you came to travel to the UK?

Tex: I had 2 brothers in the RAF, I thought I would like to come and took the chance. I was too young for the RAF; I used my Father's name. I left Jamaica on a ship that brought me to Scotland. From Scotland I went down to Yorkshire by train, where I started my training for RAF. From there I left and went to Leighton Buzzard operational training unit.

Susanna: When was that?

Tex: 1944

Susanna: When did you come to Hackney?

Tex: I come to Camden Town ('58), stayed with my brother for about three months. Then come to Hackney for a mate of mine.

Susanna: Can you think of some differences between Hackney then and now?

Tex: I would say we had more entertainment more music joints. People used to have house parties at weekends.

Susanna: What about the mix of people?

Tex: In '58 quite a few people came from Jamaica. Some in Hackney, some over Brixton side, some down country.

Previous pages, left to right: Leaking ceiling in the Kitchen at Deverill Point; living room
in 77 Deverilll Point, by Bella and Richard Callaghan; Above: the demolition of Aldbourne Point, 1996

Left: Tex Marsh with a
group of friends (Tex is
at the front left)

TOM HUNTER

London Fields is not one of London's greatest parks. It features little in the indexes of even local history books. But that's how Hackneysiders like it: no airs and graces. Eschewing the more generous landscapes of grander Victoria Park, they pour into its zig zags of a summer's day with dogs, barbecues, families, lovers, sun-starved skin, bongos, beer and bats. Guns, too. The latest police sandwich board proclaims the discharge of a deadly weapon. Highwaymen once lurked. Guy Fawkes woz 'ere.

It's not Vicky Park. It's reassuringly smaller, less like the countryside. There's no chance of escaping the noise or the press of humanity. You can see sunset, stargaze, even gather to watch an eclipse here, but you can always see a building. The modest 1960s tower blocks that anchor two corners look as if they were meant to be there; more, perhaps, than the glimpsed rows of Victorian homes, which seem exposed and shrunken without a matching terrace to face them.

There's nothing particularly distinguished about the Fields. The restored lido is walled away, the cricket pitch famously uneven and the football pitch abandoned. The bandstand and water fountain went years ago and even the graffiti looks like it's being painted over. If anything answers the missionary calling of the Victorians, who believed that urban parkland should elevate and inspire, it is the near-100 mature London plane trees that line the park's walkways. As the surrounding built environment changes, they reach firmly and confidently upward and outward. Individually, they're handsome. But together, passing the wind from one to another and presenting an ever-changing skyline as you walk by, they're a thing of grace.

Like much of what makes London London, the planes are imported; in this case, a hybrid bred from North American and

Spanish ancestors. The London plane was probably born in Lambeth during the 17th century, when scavenging and cultivating new plants from the expanding world was a glamour industry. It's by far London's most common tree, but also a mystery. It was genetically engineered less than a tree-generation ago: no one knows its lifespan. One of the earliest specimens, planted in the 1650s, is still thriving by Ely Cathedral. But London Fields' are barely 150 years old, planted around the time when the park was established in 1872.

Councillors have suggested that new generations of London planes be groomed. Arborealists say: why bother? That said, they won't reproduce. The planes themselves are largely sterile; and they're also sterile in the wildlife they foster. As non-native trees, they might look as if they were meant to be here, but only a handful of crows and pigeons would agree.

Planes give good value in the crowded city: they're modest in the reach of their roots, but expansive in their crowns and substantial in their girth. And they're city survivors: you'll recognise them by the mottled flakes of their bark, which slough off as their pores fill with pollution, pushed aside by burgeoning new skin. They've fought off carved graffiti, lofted cricket balls, dry seasons, minor diseases and Victorian smog. The only urban hazard that can kill them is the pit bull terrier, which can strip off the soft bark of saplings with their teeth.

When the crowds head to London Fields in early summer Saturday, they head for a sunny space. As the year gets hotter, they make for the shade of the planes. To lie beneath one and feel its stirring crown, or to strain to hold hands around its thick trunk, takes you up through the tips of the leaves to flirt with the sky.

GARY O'CONNOR
Talking to Moses
Photos by Cathy Lomax

I look at my watch, it's difficult to see in this light but I think it's just after midnight. It's been about five hours now and I've given up. It's remarkable that in all this time no one has heard me shouting for help and kicking and thumping on the lift door. For some reason the strip light above my head went off about an hour ago. I sit on the floor in the darkness, wedged in one corner, staring up at a thin thread of light coming in through the top of the doors. I'm stuck between floors. I know this because I prised the doors apart, no more than an inch or so, before they snapped closed almost taking off the ends of my fingers. I did this several times before realising it wasn't going to get me anywhere. This is not the first time I've been trapped in a lift. I'm beginning to wonder if this sort of thing happens to other people or is it just me. It hasn't put me off, but I do think twice before stepping into one, like I did today. In fact I came so close to not using the bloody thing – I almost took the stairs down. Down! What an idiot – who on earth takes a lift down! I won't do it again. It's not being trapped that bothers me; it's loosing time if that makes any sense. I actually don't mind confined spaces. When I was a kid I had this amazing piece of 1960s furniture in my bedroom, the sort of thing that would probably be worth quite a bit of money today. It was a large sideboard with this wild black and white Formica surface: I suppose it was meant to resemble marbling but the pattern was far too swirly and psychedelic. It had three drawers above a long cupboard space fronted by three sliding wooden doors. There was just enough room in there for me to lie down. I would take a blanket and pillow from my bed and spend ages cuddled up in there. It felt so cosy and safe. Anyway, getting back to being stuck in lifts, the first time it happened I was living in a tower block in the East End. I was with my girlfriend and we were on our way down when the lift shuddered to an unhealthy standstill. I can't remember exactly how long we were in there for but it was several hours. Caroline was becoming anxious and stressed, I was ok, it was just the stench of urine and having nowhere clean to sit that was bothering me. Eventually our cries for help were answered: a distant voice with a strong Bangladeshi accent came echoing up the lift shaft. It was one of the most bizarre conversations I have ever had. We could hear the man but I don't think he could hear us very well because he kept repeating himself. Eventually the Fire brigade arrived and after wrenching the lift up to the next floor, we were set free. What a day that was. From there we went to Caroline's car which she had parked overnight in a quiet street off Whitechapel Road, to find the window smashed in on the passenger side. My father had recently died and foolishly enough I had left some of his things in the boot: a TV, which was taken, and a box of tools. Surprisingly enough, the handgun that was in with the tools was left behind. I had no idea where my father had got the German Lugar from; it was just amongst his belongings so I took it. Shortly after, Caroline and I got married. She was never happy about the gun being in the house and persuaded me to hand it in during a firearms amnesty. I walked into the Police station in Leytonstone with the Lugar in a Tesco's bag and placed it on the desk. The duty sergeant and his colleague, a female officer, inspected the gun with great interest as I explained how it came to be in my possession, and how I would like to keep it for sentimental reasons. The Sergeant told me that I could have it registered and deactivated but it would probably be expensive. He gave me a phone number to call, wrapped the gun up in the polythene bag and gave it back to me. I said thank you and left. There aren't many people who can say that they have walked into a Police station carrying a handgun only to walk out again with it, ten minutes later, free to go about their business.

I can hear something. It sounds as if it is in the lift with me. I strain my eyes in the darkness but I can't see anything. It must be on the outside – in the lift shaft, probably a rat or something.

I keep as still as I can. I hold my breath... I listen.

We were playing hide and seek: myself, my girlfriend Louise and my friend Keith were hiding together in my parents loft. Being a teenager was so confusing, I desperately wanted to be an adult but in my heart, I was still a child. This lift reminds me of that loft. I held Louise's hand in the dark, and she squeezed mine. It wasn't long before I realised it was Keith's hand I was holding.

A small thud comes from the corner of the lift. I can see something taking shape, a tiny figure crouched on the floor opposite me slowly emerges. I'm not sure what I'm looking at; it looks like a shadow - like the shadow of a monkey.

Will you hold my hand if I ask you too? A little round face moves forward into the light.

I can't breath – my heart is thumping I'm freezing cold and I'm sweating profusely.

The grin on its face broadens as if sensing my fear.

Why are you here? The words are spoken with concern and consideration. The voice is gentle, almost feminine.

I don't know, I reply. How strange... I can't remember how I got here.

The creature tilts its head to one side and blinks. Its eyes are large and black and completely out of proportion with the rest of its face.

What do you want? I ask.

My name is Moses and this is my house.

So... err... Moses, what do you do? I sit forward and wipe the sweat from my forehead with the back of my hand.

Do? I am what I do. Moses giggles, his grin splits revealing a mouth full of gold teeth - his leathery complexion becomes a map of wrinkles and creases.

I look after things, he continues, I look after people. I like to dig holes, and put things in them, I eat things too. I break things – but I always try to fix them afterwards. I love to make music; I do this by banging things together. I watch people; yes I do like to watch people. He pauses and looks thoughtful. I don't shop anymore, because I scare the hell out of people, but I do like to take things. Moses looks at me, as if searching for reassurance, its not stealing you understand. I smile.

We sit in silence, his little hands folded in his lap.

I feel relaxed, I'm not scared anymore but I haven't taken my eyes off of him for a single moment. I can see him more clearly now, it's as if someone has turned a light on in here. I wonder if he has been in here all the time, just watching me. Maybe I am able to see him because he wants me to see him. I wonder what he wants. He must be after something.

Have you got any chewing gum?

You chew gum?

Mmm... when I can get it, Moses scratches his chin with a very long finger.

No, I reply, no I don't chew gum. Well not often.

I only want to talk, he says, with a tone of sympathy to his voice. You look like you could do with some company. You could be in here for a very long time. These words give me the shivers. I'm suddenly aware of my situation: I feel cold, hungry and tired.

Moses holds out his hand. In his palm is a digestive biscuit. There you go, he says cheerily, waving it in my direction.

I crawl across the floor of the lift and take it from him. He leans forward, the end of his tiny nose nearly touching mine.

Some people spend all their lives living in one place, he says. I can feel his breath: little bursts of warmth on my cheek. I expect a foul smell but I can't detect anything.

But this is not so true of this place, he continues. Cities are transient creatures; it's in their nature to be so. His eyes are like spheres of black glass, I can see my reflection in them.

Thank you for the biscuit, I say, retreating back to my corner. You talk about London as if it is a living thing.

It is, snaps Moses. Bricks and mortar are its bones, money runs through its veins and mankind is its flesh. When I was young it was very different around here, I was handsome back then, and a little taller than I am now, he sniggers. I haven't spent all of my life living in the shadows you know, I don't spend all of my time going up and down in a metal box either – I use the stairs sometimes. I like it by the water – do you like water? I don't really live in here, I live in the canal. Do you like water?

Er, yes. I do. I swam a lot in rivers and ponds when I was a kid. I like boats too.

There is something quite sinister about ponds and canals – don't you think? Moses regards me with a knowing look.

I suppose so, I reply. Did you say you live in the canal?

No, not really, I live under the bridge, but I don't live there, not really – I live here in this metal box with you!

All I can see are gold teeth; his mouth has taken over the rest of his face.

Is this some kind of game? I address him sternly. What is it you want from me? – I don't understand.

Moses gets to his feet. I hadn't noticed before, but he looks quite sharp in his tiny winkle pickers and his tight black suite. He approaches me. No, he whispers, this isn't a game, I'm just bored.

The lift suddenly drops and the light comes on, my vision is blurred and I feel sick.

It stops.

I sit back and the doors open. I squint as my eyes adjust to the light. I look for Moses but he has gone.

It's funny but I'm in no hurry to leave. There is a cool breeze coming in off of the balcony and the lift feels strangely comfortable. I take a deep breath and get to my feet.

As I leave I tread on the crumbs of a digestive biscuit.

MATTHEW STOCK
Urban Perception

Urban Perception explores the relationships between artist and audience, between the perceived and the undefined, between the voyeur and the narcissist through the use of video installations utilising CCTV surveillance systems.

The work examines the public in its environment, as a body in space, undermining and repositioning the natural order of private and public, displaying the intimate architecture of Regent Studios to the critical gaze of the art audience. The work aims to interrupt convention, change routine and alter the predominant narratives of the everyday.

The CCTV images are shown unedited, often showing periods of inactivity, bringing with it a sense of loneliness and sadness - compelling the viewer to participate to bring it to life.

Four CCTV cameras will be placed on the ground, first, second and third floors of the building along the outside corridors. This will track individual's movements towards and within the building itself, primarily focusing on the paths taken to get to the gallery, but will also observe numerous others. A camera placed on the floor above the gallery will track movements beyond and out of reach of which can be seen.

Two cameras will be placed within the gallery itself, these images will be delayed by 5 seconds. Allowing the viewers to interact with the work and gain a new perception of the building and the gallery environment, as well as enabling them to be both an observer of their own actions and a voyeur of others.

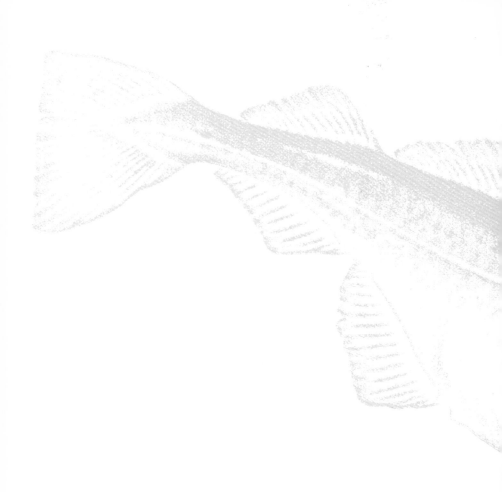

WALKWALKWALK

a chip shop tour of E8

text by Juliette Adair

Delicious & Fresh
Fish & Chips
Fried to Perfection by Experts

Gail's finding of a chip fork among the artefacts collected and catalogued on the original walkwalkwalk route was the impetus for this new project.* The small wooden fork became the key to a move away from the repetitive routine of the original route to a more extensive investigation of the E8 area. Much as those new to London explore the areas around tube stations first and only later realize how they join up, here the artists use the area's chip shops to serve as landmarks and expressions of local particularity. Each shop has something to say about the ethnic and personal character of the owner and the immediate locale. The project eschews homogenous chains and concentrates on the independent shops, their owners, employees and customers, their décor and ephemera. And, of course, their chips.

What emerges will vary with the day and the visitor, but underlying many of the stories at the time of interview was a sense of unease, difficulty, and nostalgia. The project began to look like a witness to another East End tradition under threat. A bag from the shop on Wilton Way shows a fish looking balefully at a strutting saltshaker brandishing a chip on a fork. It seems doleful in the knowledge that its end is near. Fish is endangered in the wild and as a chip shop staple. Even chips are not as cheap as they proverbially were. The chip fork as an artefact? Read Wai Lung Poon's story and weep.

There are positives though. Haggerston Fish Bar appeared to be a casualty until it reopened under new management. And someone who deserves a page of his own: the man who makes an art of serving chips. A master performer, with amazing finesse and impeccable acrobatic and comic timing; a man who knows that life is pleasant if you look after the details. Read about the remarkable act of Zekeriya Tezgel at Simply the Best Fish Bar.

This walk can be experienced as a coherent circular one or, perhaps more like life, as a series of skirmishes. What better way to feel at home in a new place than to locate your nearest chippy? Enjoy their special commemorative wrappings and other ephemera; you are creating history and bearing witness to the archaeology of the familiar and forgotten.

You can read about Gail's extensive investigation into the chip fork's possible origins on the walkwalkwalk website: www.walkwalkwalk.org.uk

Cheap as chips but who's paying?

At the Golden Star in Shacklewell Lane, Wai Lung Poon (aka Tommy) and Metta are in the mood for lamentation.

'You think they're good? No! Fish and chips are no good, not healthy. Nobody wants it.' His frustrations are many. First, the disastrous lack of taste on the part of the customers. 'They wrap them in paper – terrible! Makes them mushy. And the fish, they wrap it too. All moisture from batter goes in the paper and fish goes dry. By the time the customer gets home it's just a mess. I say, 'You want crispy chips? Just put a little salt, nothing else. Eat straightaway on a plate. But they put the vinegar, everything. Aaah."

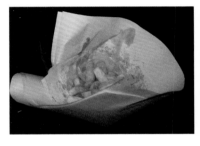

He has high standards. He and his wife peel and slice the potatoes by hand, cutting out the black bits and only partially cooking them until an order comes in. But the potatoes are sub-standard these days. Expensive too. Nine pounds a bag, even in winter. 'Don't make any money by time cut all the bad bits on a ninety pence bag of chips.'

Also the area's changed. There used to be a school next door; kids queued at lunchtime. But it closed and became an academy and the kids aren't allowed out. 'It's all black people here now. They don't care about fish and chips.'They can't afford it,' says Metta. 'It's just white people want it. And there aren't any. Not even pies sell.' Wai Lung Poon shakes his head. 'I want to close the business and buy the flats upstairs. Turn the whole thing into property that I can rent; there's no business for me any more.'

DELICIOUS & FRESH
Fish & Chips
FRIED TO PERFECTION BY EXPERTS

Golden Star, 127a Shacklewell Lane, London E8 2BE,
☎ 020 72410959
Telephone orders are welcome
Free delivery service on orders over £15
Open Mon-Sat 12noon to 12 Midnight
Sunday closed

Ming Hai
172 Sandringham Road,
London
E8 2HS
☎ 020 7254 6507
Mon - Sat: 12 - 2.30pm
        5 - 11pm
Sunday: Closed
telephone orders welcome
Free delivery service for
orders over £10

Price list:

	S	L
CHIPS	90ᴾ	£1.30ᴾ
COD		£ 2.70
SOUTHERN FRIED CHICKEN		£1 00
STEAK & KIDNEY PIE		£1.40
BEEF & ONION PIE		£1.40
CHICKEN & MUSHROOM PIE		£1.40
CORNISH PASTY		£1.40
PATTIES		£1.20
CAN DRINKS		55
SAUSAGE		£1 00ₚ
FISH CAKE		80ₚ
SAUSAGE IN BATTER		£1 15ᵥ
SAVELOY		£1.00ᴾ
CHEESE & ONION PASTY		£1.20
PANCAKE ROLL		85ᴾ
CURRY CHIPS		£1 00
CURRY SAUCE & BOILED RICE		£1.80

Performance by Zekeriya Tezgel at Simply the Best on Hackney Road.
Without looking, he grabs a can of coke from the stack behind him and
tosses it into the air. It twirls there lazily; just long enough for him to scoop
the chips into a bag. The can descends; he catches it and places it lightly
on the counter. His other hand continues to scoop chips. He looks up at the
customer for salt and vinegar clearance, gets the nod, gathers them in.
Now the wrapping: efficient and graceful as a master of origami. Then he
spins round, whips a bag off the hook on the wall, returning with a smile
and holding out the bag of chips. For the final flourish, the garnish on this
exquisite dish, he throws the coke can between his legs, over his head and
guides it gently into your out-stretched hand.

Haggerston Fish Bar

Turquoise formica and shiny trim, this pristine chippy has the feel of a 'fifties ship. There is a shrine-like corner crammed with pictures and photographs. On the end wall, high up like an icon, is a beautiful moustach-ioed man. His picture is large and framed. Loving it.'Who's that?' I ask the man behind the counter.'The owner. But not now – twenty years ago.' 'He looks like a film star.' The man nods enthusiastically.'Actually, there are two old friends of the owner. They come here and have fish and chips in the back room together.' He points through the ribbon curtain to the back room. 'They were all film stars.' There is a pause. 'You wouldn't know them, but they were famous in Turkey.'

185 Haggerston Road,
London,
E8 4HU
☎ 020 7254 8301

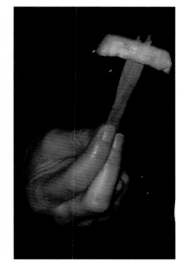

The day we put the catalogue together, I have a fever. The 149 bus stop seems like a journey to the North Pole. I phone Serena. 'I'm like the chips,' I say. 'Burning hot in the centre and freezing at the extremities.'

I burrow down in the warm wrapped poke of my duvet. It's a sort of hiding, but a sort of cosiness too. Chips are cosy. They are feverish. You want to eat them quickly, passionately, before they congeal. They can be a secret pleasure or a sociable sharing - pleasure and pain. Or perhaps that's just me, today anyway. The ache in the gut from too much oil, the thought of more cellulite. Maybe like a spring fever, they are out of season. I make it winter. I make it cold. Our breathe hangs on the air as we walk out along Hackney Road. We are wrapped up in scarves and thick coats. The bright chip shop is foggy with steam and the windows stream with the wet run off from all that frying. It feels like a sort of archetype of home.

Participate Now!

I. Dunnop talks to Tony Collins and Adam Wright, editors of Broadway Market fanzine The Eel. Main photo by Mike Talbot, market photos in text by Paul Murphy.

Tony: I don't live in E8 I live in E2. I've been there since 2002, and in a way it's The Eel that's kept me in the area. I'm part of that new wave of yuppies coming in. People make assumptions, but you don't have to conform. London doesn't belong to anybody.

Adam: When I moved here it was the leftover crusty stuff that I recognised. That's what reminds me of South London. At its roots it's got a depth and a scuzziness.

You can delve into E8. If you want to bother you can drift off Broadway Market on a Saturday afternoon and find yourself in some interesting places. You don't have to go too far. Now people walk down Vyner Street and go, 'Christ, it's rough.' I've been in London twenty-seven years, and I still go out to extreme places, still looking for something with an edge, and I can tell you that Vyner Street is not rough. It's just East London.

Knocking down the Four Aces [Dalston Theatre in Dalston Lane], that was all deliberate. There was a land grab going on, and as far as the business interest is concerned, it's a legacy they don't want to be bothered with. Their attitude is, 'Get rid of it!' In the next seven years we're going to see it all being tailormade and cleaned up. Consumed and marked and owned. Local people feel aggrieved, but there's a real problem getting them to participate.

During the struggle over Francesca's [a Broadway Market cafe bought and closed down by property developer Roger Wratten] we used to get people coming up to us going 'what are you doing supporting that bloke [proprietor Tony Platia]?' But forget the food. It's symbolic. I said be careful, have a little foresight. If this goes, that goes. Then Spirit [another Broadway Market trader fighting to save his shop] goes, and all you're left with is mythology. Then you'll be saying 'yeah, I used to go there all the time.' No you bloody didn't! Rubbish! Live now! Do something right now! Participate now, not in the future. Don't just think I'm going to pass this place in a few years and mythologize about where I was.

Tony: We've had a lot of people talk to us about their emerging anger about the Saturday market. The locals don't think it's for them.

Adam: To me it was obvious Broadway Market was going to do a version of Stoke Newington. People round London Fields had been waiting for years to be able to hang round their own neighbourhood on a Saturday.

And now it's coming you hear complaints. The locals worry that they're going to be totally overshadowed by the mediocrity of the equity scramble.

When I first moved here I was told not to cycle up Broadway Market. It was empty up there and you got mugged. Now you've got the middle classes and the new influx of students looking good on Saturday morning. You bring mum and dad up to show them they haven't fucked up giving you some money for a deposit. There's endless parents coming up to the market on Saturdays. But there's always this undercurrent of tension between the trendies and the kids from the estates robbing their bicycles.

Tony: There's loads of thievery going on on Saturdays.

Adam: The way the yuppies get their bikes nicked all the time is symbolic. They lose them and they buy them and they lose them and they buy them. It's like they're saying 'We're here to stay.' Then they come to us and complain and we make a big joke about it.

Tony: You know Ben who does the T-shirt stall? Well, when it was really hot last summer this fat kid stole something off the stall next to him. The guy on the stall shouted 'Get him, he's got my stuff'. And all these middle-class blokes in flip-flops set off after him, trying really hard but moving really slow. They couldn't catch up with him. They were going down one by one cos their flip-flops had fallen off.

Adam: We started doing a stall on the first anniversary of the market. We set up, plugged in a record player and started flogging issue one. Gave it away at first.

We try so many different ways to describe The Eel to people on the stall. You might say, 'We're reporting on swingers and bicycle thieves'. Or you could get a bit more earnest and say 'We're a collective centred around Hackney E8.' And if that doesn't work you could go, 'Well, if you want to do something for it you can get published.'

Tony: The Eel is lots of things under one umbrella. Not just the fanzine but the events we put on, which involve different people with different skills.

Adam: It's called The Eel, but it could be called anything. I was out looking for something to put on the cover of issue one, and I saw the pie and mash shop [Cooke's], and took a picture isolating the eel and the stripes on the awning. I did a mock-up, shoved it on there, and it seemed to work. It's appropriate as Cooke's is the oldest shop in the Broadway Market.

Tony: For what we're doing Broadway Market has its advantages. It's where we're based and it's quite a contained space. And it's going through a lot of changes. Part of the local thing as well is that there's so much media stuff out there, and they're all competing for the same ground. We found something that no one else was writing about, because it's so specific, so small. And it seems to work really well.

Adam: When we launched the first issue at the Percy [Perseverance], we shoved up a banner saying 'The Eel', and the guy who runs the video shop thought we were yuppies who'd bought the pub and renamed it. I asked him if he'd ever been in there, and he said no.

Tony: We were very closely associated with the Percy crowd, and there were people there who thought we were just going to carry on writing about them. But most of the stories weren't that interesting. I've lost count of the number of times I heard about how in the old days everyone used to leave their door open. That stuff wasn't really what was inspiring us. We wanted it to be more of a mixture.

Adam: What we like is the surprises. We couldn't sit in and make this magazine here. The resources are out there, you've just got to go and see what's going on and get inspired. The 'Flash Eel' [for the 'Mile of Art' event in London Fields] was a bit of a milestone. We were stumped for ideas, so I thought, 'Open access, that's a cheap way of doing it. Just put out a load of typewriters, get people writing and see what happens. Shove all the paper in a carrier bag, bring it home, and two or three weeks later get it out and go "Right, what are we going to do with this stuff?"' As it happens it worked really well. But drink being involved, some contributions were lost in the collection process.

Tony: You need fresh input. One thing we'd really like to do is go into a school or a college and get them to do half the next issue.

Adam: There's a lot of apathy round here. It's not a class thing either. The people who sit in the Percy getting pissed up every Saturday night, I put them in the same boat as the ones who do bugger all in the Dove, just play Cluedo and drink a couple of halves and talk about how the Olympics are going to make them more money. The people who interest us are the ones who are doing things. We were sitting on the stall last Saturday. And I said 'Five quid if you can flog an Eel to a girl with big bug-eyed glasses, a frock and a mobile'. And it was impossible. They'd wander over, talking into their mobiles, and you'd be in a buffer zone without any engagement. And they'd drift off. But then I suppose we did look like a couple of middle-aged Socialist Workers.

Tony: We were outside their comfort zone. Outside what they had put into their heads that they were going to do: 'Get a croissant, get a Guardian, and go and sit outside the Cat and Mutton.'

Adam: Tony's great at shoving a poker in everywhere, and I always like to keep a big spoon in my back pocket. But you've got to be careful. There's a shop in the market called 'Buggies and Bikes', and we did a joke about it being renamed 'Buggers and Dykes'. And the woman who runs it confronted us. She's going 'I'm really upset cos you're slagging off my business.' She even started crying. So there's an outlet gone. I hope we're not coming over too po-faced. We don't have a serious plan and we're not over-serious about slagging people off or putting people down. I wouldn't want people to think we were an active version of nimbies or whatever. Like I said, we want to encourage people to get out there and do things. If someone stands in front of me with some great energy, and they want to do it, then they're in.

Tony: Out of encounters like that you can create a melange of stuff. A bit like E8 itself.

This is a shortened and recast version of an interview, the full version of which is available on www.transitiongallery. co.uk/E8.

E8 Artist Biographies

Barbaresi & Round are Rachel Barbaresi and Susanna Round. They collaborate on projects examining architecture and society, producing site-specific installations and photographs. 'Thamesmead Project 2005' saw the artists twinning the Thamesmead social-housing estate with prosperous and established areas of Oxford after which much of it is named.

Emily Cole paints the urban landscape as we experience it through the eyes of public transport windows. Movement and mundanity are represented with energetic, sometimes fluorescent paint. Cole studied at Norwich School of Art & Design and was awarded a residency at Firstsite, Colchester in 2006.

Tom Hunter studied at the London College of Printing and the Royal College of Art. Hackney provides a backdrop for much of his work including one of his best known pieces, the Vermeer inspired 'Woman Reading a Possession Order'. He was recently the first photographer to show at The National Gallery with a body of work based on headlines from the Hackney Gazette.

Hilary Jack re-energises discarded or over-looked everyday objects. On-going projects include 'Turquoise Bag in a Tree', and 'Make Do and Mend', where items abandoned on city streets are repaired and replaced in the spot they were found. Jack is also co-curator of Apartment, an artist-run space in Manchester.

Gary O'Connor investigates facts and fictions, and the vulnerability of history. His work includes audio-visual installations and writing, with interviews and research into local history. He recently completed an MA in Writing the Visual at Norwich School of Art & Design and has contributed to a number of publications including 'The Alpine Adventures of Victor B' a collection of artists' fiction.

Laura Oldfield Ford produces writings and drawings influenced by Situationist theory and the socialist bent of psychogeography. In 2005 she created her own cult following under the pseudonym Laura Norder with the fanzine 'Savage Messiah' in which romance, observation, fantasy and anarchism converge in her musings on London.

Matthew Stock studied at the University of Derby, graduating in 1997. He now lives in London and has a studio at Regents Studios E8. He uses photography, video and installation, often manipulating covert CCTV footage to set up an interaction with his audience, focusing on the activities that go on in an urban setting and subverting them until they are no longer real.

walkwalkwalk was started in 2005 by artists Gail Burton, Serena Korda and Clare Qualmann. Based in the streets of East London they take the everyday urban routine as a starting point for leading groups of walkers to see and interact with the architecture, social history and physicality of overlooked corners of the city. In 2006 they produced a piece for the exhibition 'Archipeinture' at the Camden Arts Centre.